Marketing for an African Powerhouse

FATEMA G. DEWJI

FATEMA G. DEWJI

Copyright © 2018 Fatema G. Dewji
All rights reserved.
ISBN-13: 978-1727291766
ISBN-10: 172729176X

To those that light a spark in me,
You know who you are

FATEMA G. DEWJI

CONTENTS

Chapter 1	**A School Dropout and a Cheetah**	9
Chapter 2	**The Windings of My Career Path**	19
Chapter 3	**Will You Change Your Mind?**	29
Chapter 4	**Finding Our "Why"**	43
Chapter 5	**Where Success & Happiness Come From**	59
Chapter 6	**Know Your Crowd**	67
Chapter 7	**Not I, but We**	77
Chapter 8	**A Sense of Entitlement**	85
Chapter 9	**Creating Our Umbrella Brand**	93
Chapter 10	**Our Social Media Story**	99
Chapter 11	**Giving Back**	105
Chapter 12	**The Woman Who Empowered Me**	111
Notes		119

FATEMA G. DEWJI

FOREWARD

My sister, Fatema, is a walking contradiction. She is both firm and gentle.

Ask anyone who knows her, and they will tell you that Fatema has always been focused, ambitious, and driven. Whether in business or in her personal life, she has always worked hard to make a difference. Her strength in pulling through challenging times is like an iron birthmark.

I remember this particular time when she got injured. She had a golf tournament that day as well as a work presentation. How is she ever going to get through this, I wondered. I asked her to rest and postpone the presentation.

But she said, "People are relying on me to show up."

And so she showed up. For her tournament and the presentation. Her game was solid as usual. Her presentation brilliant as expected. That's my little sister for you.

Fatema has taught me that commitment is saying "yes" even on the days you don't feel good, even when you don't want to keep going.

She is not a leader only by title but one who also

inspires those around her. I have watched her build a brand and connect with people because she truly cares. In business, "Care" is a word you don't generally throw around but that's exactly what she does.

In her gentle way, she uses her heart to listen and to understand her employees, her brand, and her customers. She has managed to touch the lives of many, both through the company brand as well as her personal one.

She has inspired us to pursue our full potential.

And whenever we find bits of success, she is often the first to genuinely raise a cheer for us.

Well, I'm jumping ahead of you this time, Fatema. I'm going to be the first to raise a cheer for you.

You are an amazing colleague, sister, daughter of Tanzania. You are an inspiration to me. Keep spreading your light, in your firm and gentle way.

Hussein Dewji
Director of Sales – MeTL

Chapter 1
A School Dropout and a Cheetah

"If you give people tools, and they use their natural abilities and their curiosity, they will develop things in ways that will surprise you very much beyond what you might have expected."

— Bill Gates

Judging by the circumstances, my father shouldn't have succeeded in life.

The odds were clearly against him.

Born and raised in a family drenched in poverty, he watched his mother struggle severely with keeping the family going. Living conditions were bleak. Meals consisted mainly of rice and beans. Grandmother, or *Maa*, had to run the shop and stitch clothes for a living, all the while taking care of her husband and six children.

Maa was a clever and capable woman far ahead of her time. But the work was tearing her apart.

Even as a young teen, my father was mature enough to know his mother would crumble under exhaustion soon if he didn't do something. So he made the resolute decision to drop out of school. He headed home to work as the rusty iron gates of his secondary school in Mbeya creaked to a symbolic close.

Education, the only known pathway to Success, was

no longer an option for him.

And yet.

Hardship to Hard Work

Perhaps it was the gruelling time.

Perhaps it was the impoverished environment.

Perhaps it was watching my grandmother struggle and hearing the creak of the gates still ringing in his ears, my father worked very, very hard *every single day* to improve life for his family. Work like pumping diesel at the petrol station, and later on, driving a truck to sell produce. Seven days a week. All year round.

He never took a day off.

All my father had when starting out with his own business was a seven-tonne truck, which he'd purchased with *Maa's* help. Slowly, one truck of sweet, earthy produce grew into several truckfuls. And a small business grew into a modest, respectable trading house.

My father would take the onions to Mwanza and bring back kerosene. We traded in sugar, onions, salt, lime, textile and more. (For those of you who're new in Consumer Goods Business, here's my first piece of advice: Do not ever underestimate the significance of an onion or a bag of salt or a yard of fabric. These were and still are absolute necessities and hence, tremendous business opportunities. Respect the importance of the products you have and you're off to a solid beginning!) In fact, onions and textile fetched profits so handsome that eventually my father's business expanded into a conglomerate.

It's luck, you'd say.

No. It was his intuition grown from knowing his products well.

And an unbreakable work ethic to keep searching for opportunities, to keep loading and driving off, to keep his work in full swing always.

My father understood his products and was good at building relationships with people. He had strong intuition about things, too. For example, he would buy suit fabric in Dar es Salaam, Eastern Tanzania, and drive nearly thirteen hours up north to Bukoba to sell them at a 1000% profit margin.

Through his persistence, my father was able to grow his business and harvest it into MeTL today.

He was able to provide comfort and extraordinary opportunities for his family.

He was, despite having merely a speck of education himself, able to send his children to top schools. We all went to acclaimed, world-class universities and played sports competitively.

He gave us the best of everything.

My Father's Business Strategies

You might be thinking, with the combination of hard work and solid business strategies, it was possible for one to climb his way to great accomplishments. Sure, it would be a tough climb, but it would be *possible*. Perhaps Senior Dewji had a few marketing tricks up his sleeve?

My father was a simple business man. This was how he conducted his business 50 years ago:

He loaded his truck with salt, lime, and onions. He travelled from one part of Tanzania to another, taking turns at the wheel with his driver. Then he sold his produce.

That was it.

No business plans. No marketing strategies. All there was day in, day out, was action, sweat, and a long dusty drive under the cerulean sky.

The concept of marketing? It never once appeared in his mind.

Marketing, Huh. Who Needed It?

To be honest, Senior Dewji wasn't the only businessman who didn't care for Marketing. Most family-based businesses didn't understand the need for it.

As early as ten years ago, the Tanzanian market was very much based on a push-marketing strategy—this meant companies took their products straight to the consumer instead of waiting for the latter to *come* to them. Companies relied heavily on their distribution channel to do most of their work.

Selling a bar of soap? Don't worry if folks need it. Your distributor will plunk it right in front of them and they'll "realise" they need it.

The terms "marketing" and "sales" were generally interchangeable. When someone talked about "Marketing," they thought it meant "Advertising." (Which was known as a joke. For why would you need advertising if you already had a strong distribution channel? Why spend that money?)

Yet, multinational companies like Coca-Cola and Pepsi came into our market and blew huge portions of their budget on marketing and advertising. It baffled many of the local companies.

50 years ago, my father sat in his truck and thought nothing about Marketing.

50 years later, I sat in one of the most reputable universities in the United States and listened to my professor conclude that Marketing is FUNDAMENTAL to all business.

Marketing, Hmmh. Who Doesn't Need It Now?

It would be easy to write a book telling you your business doesn't need Marketing. Just "know your products" and "work your hardest" – like my father did.

Sure, there are certain factors to Success that will never change. And then there are some more.

Since products moved well in the distribution channel back in the days, no one wanted to give any importance to branding or advertising. This used to work for many reasons: People were not brand conscious; the buying power was low so consumers only wanted affordable products; and there was little competition in the market.

Today, as innovation spurts, competition fires up and consumers now have plenty more choices.

And this is where marketing blazes its significance.

I get it. Consumers, or rather, customers now, want to feel like they are part of something relatable, something grand. They want to feel connected to us.

However, it took a long while before our company figured this out.

A Cheetah's Race

Ever seen a cheetah sprint ahead of its herd and other animals? It runs a long way ahead, its heart drumming to the beats of the earth and its spirit slicing through the wind.

Since MeTL was one of the first companies in the market of Fast Moving Consumer Goods (FMCG) like oil, water, and wheat flour, we became market leaders. (Nifty, I know.)

We became *the* cheetah.

We became the one people in our industry watched. Our products popped up first in prospective consumers' minds. And sometimes, they were the only ones that did.

Why is that? Well, here's an easy way to understand this:

Many people know Roger Bannister as the first man to run a mile under four minutes.

Can you name the second?

How about Neil Armstrong, the first man to walk on the moon? Who was the second?

Likewise, MeTL led our market with a strong, established image. And since our products, like our Safi oil, Safi wheat flour, and Masafi water, had all along been widely accepted, we believed that any new product would easily be embraced, too—with little to no marketing required.

It was a mistake that festered into a wound in our business. The cheetah had suffered a gnash on a leg and was bleeding.

The worst part was, it didn't even realise it.

The Cheetah Trips Further

To clarify, our old products sold well because they'd been in the market long enough. It was our new products that customers didn't pick up because they didn't know they were manufactured by the team they had trusted for generations.

How did this happen?

Well typically, this is how a company markets its new product: It would run great promotions, negotiate with retailers to stock the new (and old) products in their stores, initiate Point-of-Sale displays, and encourage road shows where the company would sell the product from a truck to push for sales. Customers would generally be able to link a new product with other existing products from this same company. They would recognise the company, or the brand, behind these products.

However, MeTL was a company name they weren't familiar with. In fact, consumers often mis-pronounced it as METAL.

Why was that?

Because we did none of the effective marketing mentioned above.

Since MeTL had a strong sales and distribution team, we barely advertised any of our products. The only smidgen we did was the occasional truck branding (with images of our products splattered across and no real thought behind it). It was very random.

Equally thoughtless was our design. There was no general direction. Hardly any attention was given to colour, font, or image choices. A lot of the designs made were similar to other more popular imported brands.

Our logic was that if people liked Brand X or Y, we needed to use the same colours and designs so that they would like our products, too.

How original.

Our weak design strategy got sloppier when we created artwork for our materials. We would mix all the brands together and throw product images next to one another. There was no message, no brand identity, and hence no brand recognition.

We manufactured several brands like Safi, Poa, and Maisha yet our customers had no idea they all belonged to us. Nobody linked them to MeTL Group. We were a top national company whose customers failed to recognise!

Can you guess the next step we took?

If a product's sales remained stagnant, the easiest thing to do to beat our competitors was to slash prices.

Yep. That or giving away freebies.

Oh, sales did hike for sure. But only during the promotion. After it ended? It was a long plummet to the land of Nobody-cared-about-us-again.

There was no trace of customer loyalty. And honestly, who could blame them?

Our customers couldn't feel connected to us. We

hadn't reached out to them at all!

This cheetah had forgotten why it was in this race in the first place. For my father, it was to serve his family. In his time, we were traders and we focused on working with other traders. His approach towards work was tenacious and effective.

What about my generation? Why are we in this race? Who are we serving? Is our way working?

The ideal answer is, we should be serving our customers. Of course, it's all about humans and our communications! Unfortunately, up until this point, all we'd done was ignore them and their needs. All we'd done was plunk our products in front of them, telling them to buy, buy, buy.

This cheetah was about to feel the other animals galloping past. And it was panting on its last breath,

Chapter 2
The Windings of My Career Path

"Do not let any job that you do kill your dream. Because the only thing that can make you feel alive is your dream."

— Wyclef Jean

By now, you know about my father and our family business, how we started out, and how we developed.

Time for you to know more about me, too.

Here's the first thing I'm sharing: I grew up with an invisible sibling.

He was there before all of us were born. He was at dinner with us every day and somehow, he would sneak into our conversations some time between *kuku* and *mishkaki* and chips. He occupied our family's dreams and reality.

He was, of course, the family business.

Fatema, Always on the Move

For most of my high school summers, I interned at the family company. I would wake up early, much like men in the military do, because Senior Dewji didn't like us sleeping in. Not a fan of breakfasts, I would force down some Weetabix and banana to make sure

I had enough energy to make it to work. All this while, my mother would be watching as she ate her breakfast with much more grace.

I was always on the move. Even when I was in school, besides morning prayers and studying, I would schedule in golf, tennis, squash, and swimming sessions during my free time. Heading to the golf course for 18 holes after school or hitting 200 golf balls with my coach, *Juma*, after dinner under the stars was part of my daily routine. Even the weekends were filled with golf tournaments and swimming or tennis fun.

Yes, I said it – Fun.

I know it sounds odd for a young woman to enjoy the buzz of activity so much, but I do, I do love it. The occasional hangouts with friends were nice but I always felt slightly uncomfortable. As if I ought to be *doing* something instead of chilling. My upbringing makes me frown upon restlessness.

Which was why my internship in the finance department at MeTL nearly gave me depression. I hated sitting in one place for the whole day! Gloom cast itself all over me. I felt utterly lost and knew I would hate it if I had to do this for the rest of my life.

Someone somewhere must have heard my silent screams. For after high school ended, other opportunities began to show up.

Georgetown, Where Fate Offers Another Path

In Year 2006, I entered Georgetown University, studying Finance and Management and taking only two classes on Marketing.

Why study Business? The simple truth was I knew a lot about it. The slightly uncomfortable truth was it seemed like the only obvious thing I knew.

Fortunately for me, being at Georgetown University also granted me more options. Students have the wonderful liberty of taking subjects outside their major. This allowed me to branch out and enjoy Theology, which I almost minored in, and Politics. And since my university is famous for its School of Foreign Service, I pursued political studies, and Arabic and Middle Eastern studies.

It absolutely blew me away. Can you imagine pushing yourself out of the comfort zone and going to Egypt for three months to immerse in studying Arabic? Can you imagine attending lectures on leadership and policy given by former U.S. President, Bill Clinton? Or how about listening to rousing teachings and stories about American politics and government by the first female U.S. Secretary of State, Madeline Albright?

These precious and enlightening experiences brought me to another level. My blood ran high and wild. I had new dreams and passions to pursue.

Now, I had always expected myself to return home to help out with the family business. But towards the end of my senior year, I had made up my mind differently: I would help out at the family company for a year. Then I would switch career paths and go into Journalism, specialising in Middle Eastern stories. I wanted to write the truths of our side of the world.

So I applied to the University of Oxford to do a degree in Middle Eastern Studies.

Then I went home to help as well as to learn as much as I could.

Just One Year, Right?

It didn't take me long to find my bearings in the company. I had majored in Finance so I requested to handle the financial portfolio of the oil refinery division. Yet, this time, I was determined to make my stint different from the time during my internship. My Georgetown experiences have taught me to step out of my comfort zone and engage the other side of my brains to explore more ways in improving the running of our business.

So I did.

My tasks then were sourcing and procuring raw materials like oil and fats from the east coast to manufacture oil, soap, and petroleum jelly. Sounds straightforward, right? But my actual job role wasn't quite as clear as that. I took it upon myself to get familiar with all aspects of the unit, from Production to Sales.

It was while I was working closely with our sales team that I came upon a curiosity. They were doing a great job in making sure our products were available in the market. But who was making sure our customers picked *our* products from the aisles? (At the end of the day, it didn't matter how much we were producing if our products were not being picked up by the end consumers, right?)

Nobody could tell me. I wasn't satisfied so I paid several visits to shops that carried our products to find out.

This was the conclusion I reached: Retailers did push our products to their customers but oddly, the latter weren't able to tell that those products belonged to the reputable MeTL Group, a brand they could trust. Hence, many of them were not willing to spend money on our products!

It hit me when I saw how other companies were creating awareness of their products. Whenever I saw their advertisements, I could always connect with them. For example, Blue Band margarine made me feel I would enjoy my nutritious breakfast surrounded by the warmth of my family. Ariel and Omo assured me I could step out of home confidently, looking and feeling on top of the world. And international brands like Coca-Cola and Pepsi, besides quenching my thirst, made me feel hip and happy under the pulse of the African heat. (By the way, these were the other animals in the race. And they'd clearly overtaken us by this point.)

What about our own brand? How did it make others feel?

So-so? All right, I guess? No particular feeling. Shrug.

Finally, the bleeding wound was noticed.

I made the decision to start up a marketing division in our company. We would do this right and we would do it from scratch!

According to my wonderful plans, I would set things running then leave to complete my master's degree. Just one year, right? Yes, there was time and I was still on track.

That was seven years ago.

I'm still here.

Turns out there are certain things you can't just start then leave behind.

Taking It On

When I started off, I had no private office. I sat with colleagues from the exports division in a cramped space, and everyone assumed I was working *with* them. Nobody knew I was making plans for my marketing division. It was entirely a covert operation!

We (yes, an imaginary "we" then and in reality, a solo young woman hunched over mountains of plans to execute) would be in charge of understanding the customers, doing market research, monitoring the competition, creating brand awareness, creating budgets, setting strategy, and creating as well as executing meaningful campaigns. I hired one designer to handle all the product labels and artwork.

There were 150 products in our portfolio. I took all of them on. Like my father, I wanted to know our products thoroughly.

Besides diving into marketing our products, I took a stab at marketing our corporate side. Our website was re-designed and a 100-page catalogue was created so that our customers would know the complete list of products we have.

Wow, that was a lot of work! Was that all?

Not quite, my dear reader.

It wasn't enough that only our customers knew our products. Our staff had to know *even more* about them. So I wrote a 200-page corporate catalogue that outlined the objective of each unit and the plan for each product. (Apparently, I'd taken a fancy towards creating catalogues.)

Kind of crazy, I admit.

And it was amidst this craziness that I learned the most meaningful lesson of my life.

Anything & Everything Can Be Learnt

Wait, before we carry on, did you think all that Marketing stuff came easy to me?

Here's what I bet most outsiders think:

Sure, Fatema grew up in her family business and studied Finance and Management. She must know all those Business things. Setting up a marketing division? Easy-peasy for her!

And here's what I know most insiders thought at that time:

We Dewjis are known for our tenacity. It's only right that Fatema works as hard as we all do. More importantly, she must rise to our standards and show us results from her hard work.

Please recall that I took two classes on Marketing in university. My knowledge of it was rather limited.

And herein lies my most meaningful lesson learned:

If you want to hit your dream, your desire, your goal deeply enough, you will always find ways towards it. With the right mind-set and the right attitude, anything and everything can be learnt.

My passion in reaching out to our customers is the fundamental fuel in moving me forward.

I could have thought of my limits and hired marketing experts so I could dump all the difficult work on them.

Or, in weaker moments, I could have given up and let our family business carry on as they did. I mean, nobody else thought our lack of marketing was a problem, right? I could have just slipped away.

But I didn't. I never could.

I'm a Dewji. We do not give up or turn a blind eye to a problem.

No one wrote me a roadmap or gave me directions. I learned everything on my own from marketing books, from companies that have run successful and meaningful marketing campaigns, and most of all, from experience. Trial and error was my biggest teacher.

With gusto, I set out on my first big launch of Mo Energy, a carbonated energy drink like Red Bull but at only a quarter of its price and packaged in PET bottles. It was this launch that made me realise I'd fallen in love with my marketing work.

I was growing into a different person with many questions and further discoveries of how things work.

For example, in marketing, there is no objective reality. There are no facts and no best products. Sure, quality and price matter on some level. Yet it's not about your product having the best quality or the best price that counts the most.

Instead, it's the story you tell your customers that makes all the difference. It's the feeling that you evoke that helps you connect with them on a deeper and more meaningful level.

Everything is about perception, like how consumers perceive our products. This perception is the reality and everything else is an illusion. Each of us, from the manufacturer to the dealer, distributor, retailer, wholesaler, customer, and marketer, looks at the world through a different lens. If there is an objective truth, who would know it?

Such challenges. So much constant learning and questioning and figuring of things out. They fill me with energy every day!

I'm now officially part of the cheetah and helping it run stronger. My team of one is now a department of 25 merchandisers, designers, and market researchers etc.

Not quite my father's one-truck-into-a-conglomerate achievements.

But not too shabby, either.

Chapter 3
Will You Change Your Mind?

"Your life comes down to your decisions, and if you change your decisions, you will change everything."

— Mel Robbins

Have you ever had the intriguing pleasure of introducing a baby to solid food?

If you're a parent, this might be a familiar memory: You open the jar, dip a spoon in, and cheerily coax, "Ahhh …" as you inch the heaped mush into your baby's mouth.

You watch for reactions.

Like it? Hate it?

Baby screws up her face. Baby shivers. Baby spits the mush out with such volcanic force.

"Oh, but this is what babies love, right? The packaging looks all right, the mush ought to taste quite nice, right?"

So you try to feed her some more, nudging the spoon against her fighting tongue and trying to get as much of it into her mouth as possible.

And the tiny human erupts into tears.

What do you think happens when we try to force feed the market?

Yes, it spits right back at us.

However, unlike the defenceless baby strapped to her high chair, the market is not going to burst into a tantrum. Worse, it most likely won't give us the chance to feed it again.

Not with this product. Not even with our next.

That trust has been broken.

The Topsy-Turvy, Upside-Down Way We Created Products

One of the biggest challenges I faced working in the company was getting used to our product creation process. I found it curious that it worked the other way around.

In other organisations, there is usually a group of staff in charge of the Fuzzy Front End—the initial stage of product creation where ideas are generated and bounced around, then market trends are examined, and potential competitors are listed and studied.

The concept, now more solid, reaches the Research & Development stage, with the team leader proposing different launch strategies to the management.

Then the product is launched.

Things worked a little differently with our company.

Our management team would kick off a project by coming up with a product concept. And by "coming up," I don't mean they asked our customers for what they needed or conducted any market surveys to find out. Or anything close.

No. Our management team, based on strong gut instincts, plucked the product concept from their assumption of what our customers would need.

Not exactly divination. But more like a strong intuition about the next product we should create. Market research? No need! We played it suave.

Then after the product was created, the team would (only then) ask the Marketing & Sales department to push it into the market.

This topsy-turvy, upside-down way of Creation to Launch was challenging on many fronts. Mainly, people sometimes didn't like the product and sales fell way below our expectations.

Let me give you an example:

With our margarine, we didn't do any Fuzzy Front End. We had the concept of making margarine and went ahead with it. Production started. The margarine was distributed and placed on shelves.

Some time after, I received a call from one of our managers. "Fatema, could you please make sure you get our margarine off the shelves?"

My heart skipped several beats. *Remove our margarine? Like, entirely? What's wrong with it?*

Nothing was wrong with our margarine. The product itself was fine.

Yet we weren't hitting our sales target. We were missing it by quite a mile. Our margarine had become a huge flop! Colleagues on the production team blamed those on the marketing and sales teams, who round the game back and hurled the blame on the production team. It was a vicious cycle and we were going nowhere with it.

The margarine drama played on for a year. We put five people on this project, all of them dedicated hours and hours to help move this product. Hundreds of thousands of dollars were spent on marketing materials, distribution, packaging, and staff salaries. One whole year with all these efforts!

And still, we couldn't penetrate the market deep enough.

Again, the product wasn't *bad*. What was terrible was the way we had executed everything.

If only we'd done our market research properly at the beginning and found out more on what people wanted, what the market trends were, and what our competitors were doing so we could find another angle in before we introduced our margarine …

If only we'd worked smarter instead of making assumptions …

If only we'd tackled the issue at its roots instead of letting it grow out of our control …

We would've saved a ton of time, money, and heartache.

Our Cluelessness Continued

Without awareness of what our customers wanted, we were also often not in tune with them.

In shops, each product has its own product identification code, termed Stock Keeping Unit (SKU). Since our management team was never sure which SKUs were moving, we didn't know which products were being bought and which weren't selling too well.

Hence, we would stock up randomly, even on products that weren't in great demand. Weeks later, we would be puzzled why there was no pull from the consumers' end.

And what about those products that *were* in demand yet weren't being diligently stocked due to our ignorance?

Sounds like a scene from a black-and-white silent comedy now but back then, I was crushed.

This was hurting our brand big time.

Yes, we could have waved it aside, claiming this was generally the trend or way of business in our industry. We could have carried on, blind to our mistakes. We could have gone with the flow of our competitors and not be too bothered. *After all, this is how everybody else does it!*

But I knew we had to change. When people are not happy with your products, it reflects terribly on the entire company. They shy away from buying your other products. They stop trusting your brand.

Even after you spend a lot more time and energy in re-launching the product, the damage would already have been done. (Consumers have great memories, I've discovered.) Slowly but surely, your brand will sputter out.

But Before Systems Can Change

Minds will have to.

If you think setting up a Marketing department from scratch and pushing a product for a year without results are as overwhelming as scaling Mount Kilimanjaro, you should try changing the mindsets of people who don't understand a flicker of what you're worried about.

Brand value? What's that?

Change our product designs? Whatever for!

It's like scaling Mount Kilimanjaro in the thick of winter, with your jacket thinning and your food running as low as only two dry crackers, one of which you've lost to the biting wind. (Yes, I took some of that from Frodo's journey in the Lord of the Rings.)

Frodo had Sam, and the rest of the fellowship nearby.

I gathered myself, finished that last dry cracker, and faced the mission of changing mindsets that had served us well in the past but were not in sync with the modern times anymore.

A Single Step

"The journey of a thousand miles begins with a single step." – Lao Tzu

Friendly reminder, though: Do not crush flowers along the way with your single step.

Mindsets that have been formed for a long time are usually quite fixed while egos can be rather frail. I didn't know this at first and almost hurt my colleagues' feelings as I hurried through my "Change Mindset" mission.

For example, one of the aspects of marketing involves product designs and artwork. This part of the work used to go through the management team, which made it seem like they were micro-managing. Hey, label designs and artwork belonged within the marketing team's scope. This was our job. Not the management's, who by the way didn't have a lot of design expertise anyhow.

Nevertheless, they insisted on taking charge. Their main motto was: More is Great. In our artwork, they would order for more colours and more images. The bigger the font, the better. Scream, yell, roar!

But marketing is really about telling a clear story that connects with your consumers.

Less is More.

Clarity trumps Noise.

This was a concept our management team couldn't understand.

I remember having a lot of clashes with them when I outsourced the label designs for my carbonated soft drinks to an advertising agency. It was an agency with professionally trained and experienced designers who understood market trends. However, the management was not happy with their designs at all.

Too simple, they exclaimed.

I was frustrated and exhausted. We went round after round, with me pushing for the changes.

On hindsight, my management colleagues should be given credit. For they were ultimately willing to listen. They were willing to discuss further. They were willing to consider reaching a compromise.

They were willing to keep an open mind and heart.

An agreement crept closer after several discussions. It took a long time but at last, we were at a place where both parties were happy.

This whole episode has shown me how important it is to slow down when it comes to implementing changes in a human environment. Some people might believe that fighting your way through to get what you want is the best strategy. I could have put my foot down and insisted that the management stop interfering with the artwork. But that would have also been disastrous.

And that wouldn't be my style, either.

I prefer being nice to people I work with and maintaining respectful relationships. If you want to introduce a different concept or work structure, you have to be diplomatic and smart about it. To alter a system that is already in place, you must do it gradually no matter how frustrating it gets.

Do it in phases. Don't aim for an overthrow of the old system.

Don't butcher anyone's suggestion or idea. Don't put the ideas down the second after you hear them. Because the minute you do, egos will crack and feelings will be wounded. People will stop listening and they will shut down and rule you out.

These people have been used to a certain system for a long time. From their point of view, things have worked well. Perhaps not particularly well in recent years, but past records are evidence that their ways did work! Hence, it's tough for them to accept new and unconventional methods that go against everything they know.

Can minds be changed overnight?

I don't believe so. I also don't believe there is any point in fighting with anyone over the way we perceive things. Actions and results speak a lot louder than heated words.

So rather than rattling my management team by their shoulders, I decided to do whatever was in my control and take small steps in "showing" them the difference.

Upside-Down to Right Side Up

Following up on introducing changes, I decided to switch things a little and reversed our way in creating products for a particular detergent project. Just one project to see how it would go.

Remember how the management team would come up with random ideas on products, make them, send them out to the market, and then ask us to pull them off the shelves?

Well, this time round, I tested out my own method and began with market research.

We sought out mothers and wives who said they added Dettol on top of their washing detergents to their laundry.

"To kill bacteria. Make our clothes cleaner."

It was a simple and important wish that helped us tremendously in creating our next product.

Hey, why not add that value in our product so our customers won't have to bother with the extra step of adding Dettol?

It was something they wanted. (Not something we'd imagined they want this time!)

It was something we could produce to make their lives easier. We listened to their feedback and came up with an anti-bacterial detergent called Mo Boom. We catered it at an affordable price for the mass.

Today, it remains proudly on the shelves and is still the only anti-bacterial detergent in the whole of East Africa.

A game-changing product.

And all it took was one single effort in finding out what our customers wanted.

The management sat up and took notice.

Speak Their Language

After they saw the value of the research information my team was providing, they started making changes. I brought the product manager out to meet some of our consumers. The ladies told him their personal stories and described the difficulties they had in life and how we, as a company, could help them. The more they spoke, the more convinced the product manager was in the type of products we could create or manufacture. The type that people wanted, the type that people would buy.

We took all the market insights straight to the sales team and devised a proposal. That proposal was then presented to the management.

Now, what do you think was in our proposal? Was it a rousing, passionate story about our consumers' stories? Was it an emotional appeal on how our products could benefit Tanzanians in their daily lives?

No. In it, we created a feasibility report which showed how much market share and money we could gain in one to three years.

Hold your collective gasps, please. We do set out to bring value to our customers. We do want to improve their lives through improving the products we serve them.

But to get there, we need to convince the management that these products will in fact make us money first. We need to "speak their language" and address their main concerns (the figures) first. Only after that can we proceed with serving our customers.

Which we succeeded at that time. The management, upon reading through our research materials, approved of the proposal and production was well underway.

Change is good, but it needs to happen gradually and intelligently. Small steps will take us further in a shorter time than big, clumsy steps that wreck relationships and trust. Through understanding how people's minds work, it's easier to encourage them to attempt a new method, a new way.

And while you're at it, try coming from an angle they care about. Try convincing people in the way they'll understand. Your chances at a win-win through this "political" strategy will be much higher.

Chapter 4
Finding Our "Why"

"And I think no matter what your dream is, if you're able to find a larger purpose, a larger impact that lives beyond you, all of a sudden all of your bullshit that's holding you down becomes a lot less relevant."

— Alex Banayan

It was on one of the most unbearably sunny days in 2015 that MeTL launched our own line of carbonated soft drinks.

The heat boiled our skin. Which should have made it a perfect condition to launch our cool, sparkly, fizzy drinks. But really, all we felt was this unsettling cloud in our stomachs instead.

We were nervous because we were fifth in the market, right behind three local competitors as well as the two giants—Coca-Cola and Pepsi.

Now, competition within the soft drink business was strife to the point that even the giants had to "up their game" to make sure they didn't lose market share.

So the cheetah was fifth in place. Every strand of its fur stood alert. Its eyes were fixed on the beasts in front of it. We had entered the market late and our competition all had excellent marketing strategies.

How were we going to race past them to get to the

front of the consumers' minds?

You Need to Fail Before You Can Grow

At the beginning, we merely pushed our sodas through the distribution channel. But no one was buying. We pushed some more, and then again.

Still, it didn't work. We were selling less than 15% of what we were producing.

We introduced several flavours—Mo Cola, Mo Chungwa (an orange-flavoured soda), Mo Portello (a raspberry-flavoured soda), Malt Apple, and Malt Pineapple etc. They were priced lower than our competitors' products and came in different offerings—280ml and 400ml.

This was good, right? We gave consumers MORE products at a LOWER price, plus options.

Yet, silence rang louder than our expectations. No one asked for our products. No one was willing to try our drinks.

Undeterred, we thought we'd try again.

Our next move was to send merchandisers out to display cut-outs and danglers in the shops so that people were aware of our products. *See our posters? Go get the products!*

It was as if people were blind to us. Sales barely trembled.

We could have wailed and raged and cursed our customers for lacking the courage to try new stuff. But deep down, I knew it was because we had made no efforts in connecting with our consumers at all. Frankly, why would they want to buy from us?

Stress was high in all corners of our company. We had heavily invested in the production plant and our goal was to double production in the next two years. With such bleak results, it just wasn't possible.

I felt stuck and drained.

Simon Says

Things became so difficult that I thought of giving up. I was disconnected from our brand and there was a gap inside me. Like a hole of loss. My burning passion was being drowned by so much negativity.

During that period, when I woke at 7 a.m., I would switch on the TV. I was near mentally finished except for a last trace of persistence still holding out for...something. Hope? Motivation? I wasn't sure. Anyway, I would search for inspiring programmes to give me a boost, any boost I could find was fine.

So one morning while sipping coffee, I picked to watch a TED Talk. I stumbled across one on leadership by Simon Sinek, a British-American motivational speaker and author of four books, including "Start with Why: How Great Leaders Inspire Action."

And man, quite a talk that was. Quite the boost I

needed. Quite the jolt that brought me back to life!

In his illuminative TED Talk, Simon goes deep into how great companies distinguish themselves from the rest.

Most companies go by this sequence: First, they identify "What" it is they do—for e.g., they sell computers.

Then they identify "How" they do it—they set up this system, they create a beautiful design, blah, blah, blah.

Then they come to "Why" they are doing this. Uh, because they want to sell computers? For most companies, they draw up a blank or come up with a fuzzy reason at this stage. They have no idea why they want to do what they're doing!

In Simon's talk, he highlighted Apple, the company that uses another approach. Apple starts with "Why"—Because they want to "challenge the status quo." Because they "believe in thinking differently."

Then they go on to the "How"—Through making the computers beautiful and easy-to-use.

Last of all, the "What"—They make computers.

I'll bet when they first talked about challenging the status quo and thinking differently, they'd already had your attention. In our generation, everybody yearns to stand out and be "unique" or "different." Apple's "Why" speaks directly to our vision of who we want to be.

Following up are the "How" and "What" factors to support your budding connection with Apple and to seal the deal.

Most companies blather on about their products and what they can do. But they don't know why they do what they do, which makes it extremely difficult for customers to connect with and trust them.

This is why, as Simon also tells us, when Dell came out with MP3 players, nobody bought them. Because nobody felt connected with Dell and their latest product. Why did Dell come out with this thing? How is it a good fit for us? How is it a good fit for *me*? Why should *I* buy it?

Which led me to the most brilliant gem of an insight offered by Simon (who offers plenty, by the way):

> "People don't buy what you do; they buy why you do it."

What we do doesn't matter as much as why we do it. It never will.

And it was down to me to find out WHY MeTL does what we do.

How My Driver Almost Single-handedly Saved MeTL

> "You have a company. Why do you have that company? What is the value

> your company is offering to others
> and what do you want your company
> to leave behind when you're gone?
> There has to be a purpose for why
> your company exists beyond the
> things you make, beyond the things
> you do, beyond the money you make."
>
> Simon Sinek

Before my "Simon enlightenment," if you'd asked me what MeTL was about, I could go on and on about how many manufacturing units we had, how much oil and soap we sold, and how many metres of textiles we produced (enough to wrap the world eight times, if you must know).

It was a well-memorised chant that echoed through the company. Even when we spoke to the media, that was all everyone talked about—the macro "What" level.

While I was returning home from the oil refinery one afternoon, my driver, Esa, started chatting about one of our latest products and how helpful it would be.

"Helpful? How so?" I asked.

"The malaria mortality rates are so high in Tanzania. Your new mosquito repellent soap will keep my family and me safe."

I blinked.

Esa had moved on to how much he was enjoying our

new malt peach drink. But my conscious was still lingering on what he'd said about our soap keeping his family and him safe.

It hit me.

Our big "Why."

From the time Tanzanians wake up to the time they go to sleep, our products surround them and touch their lives in seemingly small yet extremely significant ways.

We create products that people need and enhance them, so they can improve our customers' lives. We keep families safe. We help mothers and wives run their households smoothly. We add a touch of flavour to beverages that folks under the scorching sun can enjoy. We provide good textile, so our customers have prettier and better-quality clothes.

We help people live better. This is what our brand is about.

Previously, no one understood just how much we were making an impact on people's daily lives. But in that brief exchange I had with Esa, the realisation didn't just dawn on me, it poured.

My Next Challenge

I was brimming with ideas. I knew our big "Why" now and was raring to go. I was going to tell our customers all about it.

Yet, I couldn't move. Not yet.

The biggest struggle I experienced at that point was in telling our brand story (why we're doing what we're doing) and telling it in a way that resonated with our audience. It's all very well to get pumped about your life or business purpose. But if you can't express your big "Why" with conviction and stirring power, you're still toast.

Why would our products matter? Why would anyone care to buy a Mo soda?

How could we build deeper relationships with our customers, ones that would be different from how our competitors did it?

How were we going to remind our customers that we were in their lives, that we were a part of their life stories?

Because our "Why" isn't only about us, it's about our customers. When we create a campaign, it shouldn't be about how great our products are. Rather, it must be how our products can add value to our customers. The focus has to shift from our company to our customers.

My team members had spent a lot more time in the market than I had, so I sought their advice. They gave me one heck of an idea through our energy drink. They said our customers loved it because it helped them get through a day of tedious work.

Work can be really tough over here. When there is a general feeling of losing hope and giving in to defeat, people need something to perk them up even if it's only slight comfort or cheer. Our energy drink fulfilled that role.

This was when I was inspired to create a campaign called "Usikate Tamaa."

What is Usikate Tamaa

Throughout our lives, nobody is spared obstacles and challenges. Maybe you are a young teenager struggling to get your education every day. Maybe you are a single parent working two jobs to pay for your child's education. Or maybe you are a young adult who has been told repeatedly that you are not going to make it in life.

We all face difficulties, some more intense than the others.

Usikate Tamaa is about telling these stories to the public. It is about bringing our struggles to light, about sharing them not for commiseration but for the sole purpose of encouraging others not to give up.

We believe in making a difference in people's lives.

The first step we took was to ask our customers to share their stories, their intimate stories of how they didn't lose hope despite the challenges hurled at them. And how they gradually stepped out of their personal darkness into beams of success.

This would in turn inspire others on their paths.

With this vision in mind, I set out to find a story that could echo the spirit of Usikate Tamaa perfectly. That was when I learned about Shetta's.

Born in the city of Dar es Salaam, Shetta (whose real name is Nurdin Bilal Ali) grew up dreaming of becoming a musician. However, even though he believed he was talented, people thought he would never get anywhere. Having an artistic dream was considered lofty and luxurious.

Not possible, others would tell him time and again. *Stop dreaming.*

Shetta was not one to lose hope so easily. He used to live with a big musician in the country, Dully Sykes, and from there, worked his way into the music circle through washing cars and dishes. Like my father, Shetta was not afraid to work hard. He was not reluctant to start from the low rungs to climb to where he wanted to be.

And eventually, he did. Naysayers and life's disappointments couldn't mute his passion. He is now one of our most successful musicians, with several songs topping various music charts in Tanzania and even across the whole of Africa.

His personal story of grit and perseverance inspired me and I knew it would inspire millions more. Who else could launch our campaign better than Shetta? I reached out to him and he agreed.

Excitement emitted from every pore of my body. I was so engrossed with this project that my team and I did everything—from brainstorming on the branding and the artwork to filming and directing the ad for the campaign ourselves. We spent $400 for an ad that went viral.

What made it go viral?

The storyline. It was about a young man doing hard labour painting walls who then rushed to different interviews, hoping to get a better job. He faced disparaging treatments from potential employers. He stood through humiliating remarks. He was willing to work hard (we saw him painting walls under the sun), yet nobody would give him a chance.

And he broke down.

Who couldn't relate to how he was feeling?

Then a friend offered our energy drink to him. It wasn't just an energy drink that cooled him off. It was a drink that was like a friend, that comforted him then restored his spirits. So he tried again and went for one more interview.

Tears of disappointment became tears of joy when he got the handshake he'd yearned for.

And who wouldn't smile and cheer at that? Our audience was hooked because we had told their story in the ad.

Soon after, we were unstoppable. People would sing to our jingles and share their stories on social media. We've since created a community where people can share their personal stories and help one another. We're now a genuine part of their stories.

This is Usikate Tamaa.

And we're only just beginning.

Not Merely Soda Sellers

We are more than that.

Through our Mo brand, we want to share feelings, we want to spread hope, we want our drinks to pass on physical energy and emotional strength.

When our customers take a sip of our soda, we want them to feel their fatigue and despair fizzing off their bodies and minds. We want them to feel less lonely in their struggles. We want them to be reminded that they are surrounded by others' support and love.

We also want to respect and acknowledge everyone's inner strength and perseverance. We want to honour these ordinary folks. We want to give them a place to share their voices so others can hear them and feel inspired.

Outside the company, finding our "Why" has helped us reach and touch our customers.

Inside the company, it has also led to several business results:

First, we get to produce more flavours that our customers are excited about, like Coffee Malt, Mo Pineapple, Mo Lemon Mint, and Vanilla Cola.

Second, since customers have responded warmly towards our flavoured drinks, we get to push for Mo Cola too.

Our cola drink used to be a huge splinter on our side because we could not compete with the giants—Coca Cola and Pepsi. These two competitors have been around for so long we couldn't penetrate the market as deeply. Also, they have enormous budgets and a strong distribution channel dedicated to only one product while our budget must be spread across hundreds. Hence, we had very little market share with Mo Cola.

To pull out this splinter, we decided to attract consumers through our other soda flavours, flavours that aren't available from other companies. This strategy called Flanking Marketing (think of it as attracting customers from the flanks of your core product, i.e. those "side" products) has worked beautifully. Drawn initially by our distinctive soda flavours, consumers are now confident in us and are more than willing to try out Mo Cola. We recently re-launched our cola and its smashing success has allowed it to stand right beside the two giants!

Third, because of our successful campaign, Coca-Cola and Pepsi have to raise their game as well. This competition has pushed everyone in the soft drink industry to become more innovative in their marketing.

Creativity sparks all around.

An Interesting Side Story on Competing with Others

It's difficult to ignore your competitors. Especially when you are in a desperate race to the top. But sometimes, we need to adjust our lens and see more clearly what we are competing against.

When we stopped worrying about what the giants were doing, we were able to take another shot at the big picture. And we did better.

In a similar case, when Roberto Goizueta took over as the CEO of The Coca-Cola Company in the 1980s, he was handed the immense task of surpassing Pepsi in sales. As their biggest competitor, Pepsi was eating away their market share.

The Coca-Cola executives were obsessed with Pepsi and bent on increasing their market share 0.1% at a time.

Roberto, however, made the decision to zoom out of their focus on Pepsi.

He adjusted their lens. And zoomed in on the whole beverage market instead. Water, coffee, tea, milk, and juices were their competitors, not just Pepsi. In that strategic move, he changed the entire game plan.

He asked his team how much fluid an American took on average per day.

"14 ounces."

What was Coca-Cola's share of that?

"2 ounces."

Roberto told them they needed a larger share of this market instead. He wanted the public to reach for a coke whenever they felt like having a drink.

Hence sprouted the coke vending machines on every street corner.

Coca-Cola's sales took a quantum leap.

Big lesson here: Adjust your lens once in a while. There could be a bigger picture you're missing.

Chapter 5
Where Success & Happiness Come From

"What counts in life is not the mere fact that we have lived. It is what difference we have made to the lives of others that will determine the significance of the life we lead."

— Nelson Mandela

Back in 2006, on a beautiful May morning, I walked into a lecture room in Georgetown University and waited for my first class on Management.

My professor, Robert Bies, was a bespectacled and warm gentleman in his fifties. His hair barely touched his shoulders and his eyes emanated kindness. He smiled and began his class thus:

"Success and Happiness come from finding a purpose that is greater and higher than yourself and making a difference in the world you live in."

Safe to say, I was certainly not expecting him to start a Management class with life philosophy!

But there we were. Professor Bies started every class with his trademark smile and this beacon of truth. Out of six semesters of Management classes, I signed up for four of his. Given my excellent attendance record, I must have heard that opening approximately 168 times! (Who knows, perhaps I'd turned up *just so* I could hear those delicious lines that would later manifest into a life motto?)

So what does it mean to find a purpose that is greater than yourself?

Put simply, it is to be less interested in yourself and more interested in the world around you.

CARE is as Important as CAREER.

MeTL has found its "Why." What about mine?

By 2015, I was working 12 hours a day, five and a half days per week. I loved my job and was deeply passionate about my work.

However, my life was on autopilot. I would wake up, go to work, go to the gym, then hang out with my friends without feeling truly fulfilled. At work, I would claim huge achievements yet there would be emptiness lingering in my soul. When I went running outside, a part of me was just not alive. On holidays, I would buy things that didn't satisfy me.

Something I desired was lacking. I knew I was put in this world *for way much more!*

Days passed with me feeling "fine." But I didn't want to feel "fine." I wanted to feel fulfilled and happy.

This happiness I was looking for didn't come from taking holidays or shopping trips. It didn't come from hanging out with my friends either. I wanted happiness that lasted.

All the Aminas Out There

What Nelson Mandela, the first black president of South Africa, said about the significance of our lives burned a question right through me: *What difference can I make in the lives of others?*

On one of my regular visits to an orphanage, I found my answer.

I had become close to a girl called Amina, who lost her mother to cancer and her father to a car crash when she was seven. I saw what a struggle it was for her to find money to do basic things like go to school, get running water, and buy clothes. Things I never had to think twice about because I was so blessed.

How many Aminas are out there waiting to catch a break, I wondered.

Growing up, I was fortunate enough to attend schools of the highest calibre and play golf competitively – a costly sport. I am so grateful that I have a father who always pushed me to work hard, train hard, and stay disciplined.

Yet how many girls in Tanzania are given similar opportunities and support?

Or how about for a moment we strip away the privileges and ask truthfully, how many girls are given the basic opportunities and support to *simply* finish their education?

The Birth of Educate, Empower & Inspire

One of my heroes is Dr. Muhammad Yunus, a Bangladeshi social entrepreneur, economist, and founder of the grassroots Grameen Bank. He is known throughout the world as a pioneer of the microcredit concept, which offers to improve the lives of impoverished people, mostly women, through small loans with affordable interest rates. Dr. Yunus and his Grameen Bank were jointly awarded the Nobel Peace Prize in 2006.

Dr. Yunus sees poverty as a circumstance that deprives people of all human value. Microcredit then is both a human right and an effective means of emerging from poverty. By issuing micro loans to those who do not have access to traditional credit and teaching them a few basic financial principles, Dr. Yunus claims that they can generally break the vicious cycle of poverty and begin managing their own lives.

A chance at a new life.

Like all great figures in history who have lived for a cause bigger than them, Dr. Yunus's passion lies in helping people born in the most unfortunate rung in society.

And I aspire to do the same.

According to Human Rights Watch, more than 1.5 million adolescents in Tanzania are prevented from attending secondary schools. Obstacles include a lack of proper schools in rural areas, an exam that limits access, a government policy that forbids pregnant or married girls to continue their studies, and poverty.

Despite the Tanzanian government's decision to make secondary education free, many families are still unable to afford school uniform, books, or transportation. Furthermore, minimal efforts have been made to make sure students are safe from abuse in school. Hence, students often choose to drop out.

Without proper education, what chances for a promising career do these teens have?

And what about girls who are forced into marriage? According to a national survey on child marriages, 37% of girls in Tanzania are married before they turn 18 years old. They could be as young as 14 and if they are tested pregnant, the government would have essentially ruled them out of any possibility of a bright future.

Young girls are definitely the most vulnerable group of people I feel the urge to help. I've decided my life purpose would be to empower them, as well as all women and young people everywhere, in using their gifts, their talents, and their strengths to get themselves out of poverty and into better-quality lives. Through social media and my YouTube channel, I want to aspire them to be the best they can be.

A chance at a better life.

The best life they can get.

Dream Bigger

It was around this time that I was asked to give speeches at different events. At one of them, I was invited to talk about my career, my position as the Director of Marketing at MeTL, and my position as the founder of Educate, Empower and Inspire.

But something steered me in a different direction that day. Before I went into my "career" and "positions," I told them a story.

The story of Inky Johnson.

For those who don't know, Inky Johnson is an American who used to dream of becoming a professional football player and one day join the National Football League (NFL). Inky had had that dream since he was seven years old. Every single day, he would do drills and practice even when no one was watching so he could one day make it big.

He was tired of the bad neighbourhood he was raised in. He did not want to share a bed with 14 other people anymore. And most of all, he wished to inspire the kids around him, to influence them towards the right dedication and work ethics. He wanted to help get them out of their dire situations, too.

One afternoon during a game, Inky's life changed. A routine tackle turned into a life-threatening tragedy and he was told he could never play professional football again. He was eight games short from being drafted into the NFL, eight games away from becoming a multi-millionaire, eight games from not having to worry about missing a meal again.

Was that the end of his dream?

Yes.

It was the end of his NFL dream. But Inky was not done.

He picked himself up, continued fighting the daily pain and physical challenges, and is now using his story to inspire millions on leadership, teamwork, and perseverance. During an interview, he was asked how it felt when he realised his dreams would never come true. Inky responded that he was "embarrassed" because he realised he had spent his whole life dreaming of just becoming an NFL player.

He realised how SMALL his dream had been.

I was invited to talk about my career and this was what I'd told my audience:

"That is what most of us do: We limit ourselves. We believe that if we can only make this much money, if we can only get this position, we would be happy.

But what happens when Life redirects us?

We want something so bad but things don't always work out like that. We are too busy chasing these titles and these positions that we forget to chase fulfilment. We forget to make an impact."

To make an impact.

To have bigger dreams than fancy-sounding job titles at work.

To care and help raise others. I knew then that that was the lasting happiness I wanted.

The Power of Caring

I've since discovered a new side to myself, a side that takes great pleasure and pride in watching others thrive and succeed just as much as I do in my own life. There is beauty in helping others. It makes you feel good but more importantly, it allows you to grow and add value to yourself.

Invest in others and you'll be investing in your personal growth.

Caring for one person can bring so much power to the one being cared for as well as to the carer. This value in my personal lifework also seeps into my marketing work for the family business. The desire to help people has pushed me towards directing my focus towards humans instead of goods.

Mainly, I've stopped emphasising so much on merely selling my products. Instead, I'm building more trust with my customers and stronger relationships with my colleagues. I know that if a business does not care about its customers and employees, it cannot succeed.

Which brings me to this next stage of understanding my customers and engaging them deeper.

Chapter 6
Know Your Crowd

"To add value to others, one must first value others."

— John Maxwell

Remember my first case of market research?

We had found out that women liked adding Dettol to their laundry and so we created an anti-bacterial detergent for them. Sounds uncomplicated and thoroughly feasible. It was all about understanding our customers' problems and helping to solve them.

Later on, more incidents led me to the unshakeable belief that market research is key in building stronger grounds with our customers. Simply because it helps us understand what works for them and what doesn't.

And the person who showed me the way in one particular case of "what doesn't" was my caddie.

Meet Bomba

Bomba has been my caddie since I was six. He has watched me grow up. He has watched me take on various challenges on the course, at school, and now at work. Bomba is the true epitome of hard work. He works as a caddie while his wife runs the shop from home selling commodities, including our products.

I look up to Bomba. Maybe it's because the way he works so hard to send his children to the best schools, the way he tells me he never wants them to struggle through Life like he has had, the way he tries to get them educated, all remind me of my father.

One sunny Sunday, while on the golf course, I chatted with Bomba and thought I'd do some market research at the same time. (I know, I'm quite the multi-tasker.)

Knowing that he and his wife usually stock their shop with lots of goods, I asked which brand of detergent his customers preferred.

"*Mama*," he called me out of respect and said, "they prefer the small bag."

The small bag? We didn't carry any brands that came in smaller packaging.

That was when Bomba told me the full story. The truth was that our customers had been getting smaller, unmarked bags of detergent.

At that time, we were selling detergent in 10 and 15 kg packs. Since the purchasing power in Tanzania is low, most folks are not able to buy regular household items in bulk. The women who went to our retailers did not have the means to buy such big bags of detergent powder for the whole month.

Hence the solution was to ask the shop keepers (like Bomba and his wife) to open a 15 kg bag, scoop out some detergent into a smaller bag, and buy that.

A smaller bag with no logo, no brand name.

Our end consumers didn't even know which brand they were buying.

This affected us in many ways, including my missed opportunity of branding. But more importantly, our customers were not getting what they needed, which was small consumer packs for them to use for short periods of time within the budget they could afford!

Another concern was that not all the shopkeepers were reliable and trustworthy like Bomba and his wife. Some would deliberately scoop less detergent yet charge the same price. Our end consumers could not fully benefit.

It was time to change.

I decided to launch 500 gm and 1 kg packs. It would be just right for our customers to spend on without getting cheated. Also, the hygienic quality of the powder would be fully in our control. For one, shop keepers would not be able to add other mixture into our powder. For another, our bags wouldn't be opened for smaller distribution, hence making it less likely for the remainder to be contaminated in the warehouse.

If it hadn't been for market research (on the golf course!) and our efforts in uncovering actual consumer behaviour, we wouldn't have been able to provide Tanzanian wives and mothers with what they really needed. We wouldn't have played a more significant role in their lives.

Branching Out

As demonstrated above, one good use of market research is to help us understand our consumers' needs.

Another is to branch our products out.

Here's another example of how we did it:

In the past, our soap was a bar for multipurpose usage. This means people used one bar to shower, wash clothes, and cleanse anything else. It felt rather like what a family in the stone age would do: One bar for everything!

After conducting interviews and grasping our consumers' different needs, we began creating soaps for various purposes. For example, we now have beauty soap with fragrance specially for women, luxury soap for hotel use, medicated soap for killing germs, and Mo Mosquito Repellent, a bathing soap that wards off insects. By introducing different soaps, our consumers have more variety to choose from.

And who doesn't enjoy choices?

How I Go About Marketing

In marketing, I believe in a 360° approach. To stay in the foreground of your customers' mind, you have to be able to engage all their senses.

This means my campaigns are usually all-rounded. I organise TV commercials, radio jingles, billboards, social media promotions and more to get right in front of our consumers.

Why so much work?

I want them to see and hear us frequently. When husbands are driving, they will see our billboard and be reminded of getting detergent for their family. When mothers or grandmothers are at home, they will watch TV or listen to the radio. Once they see or hear our ads, they might be curious to try out this new oil product. For the younger working adults, they are likely to come across one of our social media posts or ads on our beauty soap.

It's all about targeting where consumers might be and then placing ourselves right there with them.

Who Buys the Margarine

One of our most effective 360° marketing campaigns is for our margarine.

A little background here: The two biggest margarine brands in Tanzania are Blue Band and Prestige. Since they have been in the market for so long, no one wanted to buy our margarine.

What did we do?

Well, our first task was to find out who the decision maker in an average family was when it came to buying margarine. (Are you thinking it must be the mothers?) Through careful market research, we found out that it was actually the kids who consumed the most consumer pack margarine!

We tweaked our marketing efforts and targeted at involving the kids. A campaign called "Mo Margarine Star" was launched, with the plan to get kids to demand our margarine by name.

We created a radio jingle and encouraged parents to ask their kids to learn it. After reciting the jingle, they could upload their performance on social media and tag it with "#MoMargarineStar." Ten kids who recited this jingle best would win a one-year academic scholarship.

Which parent wouldn't want this?

And which kid wouldn't have fun doing this? It was win-win-win for everyone.

To get this campaign across, we posted ads on TV, radio, newspaper, and social media; we printed flyers and billboards; we even planned for ground activations where our team, fully decked in Mo Margarine T-shirts and caps, would go to schools to promote.

The idea was to serve a jingle that would become a song the kids would remember for years to come.

This way, my brand would be ingrained in their mind.

The outcome? Our cheerful and catchy song really caught on! We had kids dancing and singing to the tunes and sending us amazing videos. Everybody had a blast!

Taking It Another Step

So far so good. However, there's always one further step we could take to enhance the whole customer experience.

Getting your senses involved does not only mean seeing and hearing about your products, it means connecting with feelings and thoughts, too.

In the past, we merely placed our product images in newspaper ads and on trucks. It was literally just product artwork with their SKU and size details. This is still the norm for a lot of companies in Tanzania.

From a customer's perspective, these ads were in no way catching my attention or speaking to me. I wanted ads to tell me a story, to grab my attention. So I decided to change all my truck branding to make sure that our ads featured people using our products and showed what they were feeling.

For our margarine campaign, I added a little humour by showing a child do a funny face while thinking to himself how many slices of bread he was going to eat with the margarine. The concept behind it is, "If you try it, you will want more." Both the human and comical aspects achieved two things: Grabbing attention and allowing people to relate to the boy's innocent sense of fun.

Ultimate Act

Finally, my 360° approach cannot be pulled off successfully without this last step.

Have you had the experience of seeing a beautiful dress or a scrumptious-looking snack in an advertisement and felt something within you click?

The prints. The cutting. How you'd look in that dress. Or the crunch. The filling oozing out in your mouth, which curves into a most satisfying grin.

"Man, I must check that out!"

Yet when you get to the store, the salesperson/clerk shrugs and tells you that the item isn't available. He then carries on clacking price stickers with his label gun.

How would you feel?

Annoyed with the clerk and the store? *How could you not have what I want?*

Pretty soon, that annoyance will grow into a barrage of complaints at the company behind the product. *Why post an advertisement to entice me then lack the foresight of stocking up in stores? Why raise my interest then dash my hope? Why make me feel unsatisfied? I feel foolish and played!*

The last step of a product launch is tremendously importantly—making sure that when all the senses have been connected through our ads, our products are well-stocked up in stores. So that people who are ready to buy won't have to struggle to find them.

I Learned This the Hard Way

When I launched my Mo Beauty Soap, I made sure that everything on the marketing side was taken care of. However, I started getting lots of complaints from my customers that while they saw the ads almost everywhere, the product was poorly distributed and nowhere near them!

At that time, I had not examined the availability of the detergent closely because I had thought that was the sales team's responsibility. Not mine.

This taught me a harsh lesson. First of all, if one part of the equation doesn't work, it has an effect on everything else. This is not only about making sales, but about working together seamlessly.

If there is a production problem (say, our production pace cannot meet the demand from the consumers), it will chip away all our marketing efforts. What was the point of all the ads if our customers couldn't get what they wanted?

Second of all, it taught me that situations like this can create a reverse effect on brands. If a customer does not have easy access to your product, it can frustrate them and ruin their impression of you.

From that lesson on, I promised to make sure I was in sync with the sales team before executing my marketing plans.

Yes, it is one more task to do. But my customers are absolutely worth it.

Chapter 7
Not I, but We

Talent wins games, but teamwork and intelligence win championships.

— Michael Jordan

What do you think is the top reason behind a company's success?

Is it creativity? Is it production power? Is it hired talents?

I'm more inclined to believe in the power of teamwork. When I have my one-to-one meetings with unit heads (whether it's for my wheat flour or my carbonated soft drinks etc.), I make sure that I invite the respective marketing teams, sales teams, and most importantly, the heads of production.

You might wonder, what does production have to do with marketing?

Throughout the years, I've found that when the whole company is not in sync, it stirs up many problems. And when that happens, *everybody* loves to play the "Blame Game." For example, the marketing team would blame the sales team for not distributing the products well enough or not stocking them frequently enough. The sales team, on the other hand, would blame the production side for not manufacturing enough or not resolving specific production flaws, like adjusting the saltiness in our margarine or checking the shape of our soap bars, quickly enough.

Fingers would point. Shouts would ring out. And tempers would flare across the room, scorching everyone's mood and energy. There would be no progress, no help at all.

What Does Help

Bringing everyone together, on the other hand, has helped MeTL achieve many things.

First, it has given everyone (and I mean everyone from the head of a unit to a junior designer) an opportunity to be heard and included.

How is this important?

Being listened to is an innate human desire. So are being appreciated and validated. Everyone has something to contribute and everyone yearns to be heard. When people work together and ideas are allowed to flow freely, there is greater productivity and team unity. There is a stronger sense of "We're in this together. We've got each other's back."

Second, it holds all of us accountable for our roles. At such meetings, there is no way anyone can dodge responsibilities or use the "Well, I didn't know that" excuse.

This was challenging at the beginning because there would be certain managers putting their hands up and exclaiming this or that department had nothing to do with them.

With quiet patience, I would listen while they vent. When emotions flare up, even if it's one-sided, it is always wiser to stay calm. Suck it up, as they say on the streets.

Then handle the situation when things are less heated up.

"Nobody is blaming you," I would reassure them privately after the meeting was over. Once their expressions and body language tell me that their storm has passed, I would then explain what we were all trying to achieve together. That to get to our best results, sometimes we would have to set our egos and differences aside.

Not the easiest conversation to have, but certainly a necessary one!

Good leaders lead by example. I started taking a keen interest in other aspects of the business. If the production team was having difficulty on their end, I would find ways to troubleshoot the issue. Many times, I had to give motivational speeches about how important it was for everyone to work together, that their job roles sometimes had to be fluid to make sure that the task was getting done and done well.

It wasn't about "my department" or "their department." It was about *our* company, *our* products, and *our* customers.

Break or Make

It was hill after hill of trials. After doing this with different units in the organization, I found that the carbonated soft drinks plant had the best team synergy.

Mind you, this was not the case at first. Communications between the production and sales teams of our sodas had been practically zero for years!

When our soft drinks started doing really well, we didn't have the capacity to produce more. We had to buy a whole new line to meet the crazy demand. However, the production team wasn't aware which flavours were in high demand and which weren't, so they kept putting out sodas according to the previous ratio.

Flavours that were not that popular (like our Lemon Mint soda, for example) moved slower than snails.

Then on the other side, we had flavours that were highly demanded by consumers (like our Passion and Portello flavours). Yet they were not getting produced quick enough!

I was exasperated by this glaring lack of communication. Immediately, I called for a meeting to make sure that the sales team was updating the production team on what flavours made our consumers happy.

It took months of drilling home this concept of communication before things finally improved. (Yes, months! People were that reluctant to talk to one another.) I created an email thread where everyone involved was CC'ed and held accountable. It was a frustrating period but I knew getting tight would get me nowhere.

So I took the other approach.

I talked to them about the value of working together. I showed them figures we could achieve if communications improved.

Slowly, egos stepped aside. Results trickled in and people were more willing to work together. Only then did our fast-moving flavours get produced perfectly according to the sales demand.

Communications and team efforts can certainly break or make our success.

These days, I take one step further in communicating with my team members. Besides the daily updates, I also let them know my appreciation for their efforts. When anyone does well, I always send out an email telling them what a fantastic job they've done.

When I started out, someone did that for me. It made me feel truly valued and I want to make sure to pay it forward.

Another Proud Moment

Take our "Under the Cap" promotion as another example.

At the end of 2017, we decided to increase the capacity of our water lines. So we introduced a new campaign called "Pindua Ushide" which was set to run from December, 2017 to March, 2018. It was an Under the Cap promotion (UTC), meaning that whenever someone purchased our water, they could check under the bottle cap to see if they'd won a prize.

Prizes included Maji Bure (Free water) and cash ranging from 1,000—100,000 Tanzanian shillings. If a customer won free water or 1,000 TZS, 5,000 TZS, or 10,000 TZS, they could collect their prizes from the shop keepers.

Bigger sums would have to be collected from the A-One Products and Bottlers team (a MeTL Group subsidiary and Tanzania's leading producer of water and drinks) at their factory. Winners would be photographed collecting their prizes and they would make the news. We wanted everyone to know that this was an authentic campaign so more would join in.

So our teams went to work.

The production side took charge of the cap bottles, making sure prize announcements were lasered and covered with a small sticker.

The marketing side worked on the advertising,

including liaising with billboard companies and radio stations, creating campaign copy and design, radio jingles, TV ads, as well as social media promotional materials.

The sales side took care of distributing marketing materials like posters to the shopkeepers so consumers could know about our campaign. As well as stocking up our water.

It was like an orchestra coming together to play a beautiful symphony. Sure, there was a hiccup along the way. That small sticker that was supposed to hide the prize surprise under the bottle cap kept peeling off on its own. But we managed to fix it. Our launch ended up slightly delayed (yes, do not underestimate the effect of a small peeling sticker) but which world-class orchestra/company doesn't face hiccups?

It was the way we dealt with everything that spoke of our standards. And this couldn't have been accomplished without great communications and team(s) work.

If the production side hadn't fixed the bottle cap issue or if they hadn't produced enough water for this campaign ...

If the marketing side hadn't come up with a campaign that attracted the audience ...

And if the sales side hadn't responsibly worked with shopkeepers in distributing our posters and then stocking up on our water ...

Pindua Ushide wouldn't have succeeded. Our water

wouldn't have moved much. And people wouldn't have won prizes.

Goodness!

The highlight came when we learned that our water competitors were slashing their prices. Our penetration had been so amazing they felt seriously threatened.

I couldn't have felt prouder of my teams. Our customers weren't the only ones winning rewards here.

Chapter 8
A Sense of Entitlement

"Without those really hard times you just don't get the euphoria on the other side."

— Lori Harder

As a leader under 30 years old who's handling such a large portfolio, I face questions and judgments every day.

You got handed this position without even working for it. How can people respect you?

Do you even know enough?

We know you have passion and gusto because you're young. But how far can these carry you?

Many family businesses choose to hire one of their own blood relatives for a high and important post because of trust and because they want to keep the money within the family. As such, these people who seem to have "risen to the position" must prove themselves to the watching world time and time again. Sometimes, I think we have to work so much harder because of this.

Every day, my brothers and I wake at dawn and show up at the company early to set an example. And to send out the message that we are not entitled brats, that we have our work ethics, too.

I know for a fact that there are thousands of people who are capable of filling my position and possibly doing better than I have. I work and manage people who are twice my age and have tenfold my experience. Many of the CEOs of our units were former Coca-Cola, Pepsi, or Unilever employees who had worked for other well-known multinational companies. They came with ideas and strategies to add to MeTL.

Which is why I highly respect them.

And which is why I always remind myself to stay a humble learner.

One of the most fundamental principles I work by is Respect through Relationship Building. Instead of walking around like an entitled lass, I've chosen to take the opportunity to learn from people I respect. I always believe that if you want to learn more, achieve more, and get better results, you have to be humble. You have to respect others. You have to build genuine relationships.

When you inflict fear in someone or when you are unapproachable, you are actually creating a wall between yourself and your employees. They would be either too scared or not bothered to tell you if there was a problem or if they had a great idea.

But when you choose to listen and respect them ... a world of improvement opens right up.

Fatema the Spy

Once, I had the most fruitful conversation with one of my sales managers. He was the one who "enlightened" me about the state of our beauty soap.

For a long time since we rebranded our beauty soap, the sales team had hesitated telling me the real problems that were causing the lack of sales. They were under the impression I would call the production team and start yelling. (Me, yell?) Which would then cause the production team to point at and swerve unnecessary unhappiness back to the sales team.

My sales manager told me he'd gone to the market and discovered that our soap needed modifications. The customer feedback he'd gotten was that the scent wasn't strong enough, the design was bleh, and the soap didn't produce enough lather.

For other products like our wheat flour, the feedback was that the quality wasn't too good.

I was impressed.

By one trip to the market, my manager was able to give me so much more information. Curiosity drove me to visit the market myself and engage with customers. Why not find out the truth about my products and learn what I could to help improve my business?

So I went undercover as a customer and asked the shopkeepers about our products. What I discovered was that:

- People absolutely loved my sodas but weren't happy with the distribution of some other items.
- Quality-wise, our products scored well. But awareness-wise, they didn't. (Interesting.)
- There were some issues with pricing as well. (Good, now I'd know what to start fixing!)

Because of that one conversation with my sales manager where I listened and paid attention, I was given more directions towards what wasn't working.

Because I took the dive into the market and respected my shopkeepers' and customers' feedback, I gained so much more in return!

To get more people to open up like my sales manager did, as well as to help them listen to what I've gathered from the market, I've learned to communicate effectively through gratitude and encouragement. For instance, after my trip to the market, I called for meetings and invited everyone from the production team over. I gave them the feedback collected from the market (and not from the sales team) so the production team would know this came directly from our customers.

First, they learned about the areas we were doing well and were told how proud and appreciative I was. Then they were fired up with encouragements on facing the other challenging areas and how we could all work together to make our products go from Less-than-Ideal to Good (and then to Great).

They were willing to listen and respect what our

customers were "telling" us.

And this world of improvements, from our product quality to our work collaborations, opened right up.

Simon's Styrofoam Cup Story

At an Usher's New Look event, Simon Sinek told the story about a Former Under Secretary of Defence giving a speech at a conference. (This is a true story, by the way.) The Former Under Secretary was up on the podium, holding a cup of coffee. Some time into his presentation, he took a sip, looked down at his Styrofoam cup, and smiled.

He told his audience that the year before, while he was STILL the Under Secretary, he had been invited to that same conference. He had been picked up from the airport and driven to his hotel then later to that same conference location. And he had also been offered coffee.

In a ceramic mug.

A year later, retired from his job position, he got a Styrofoam cup.

The lesson he'd learned was that the ceramic mug was never meant for him. It was, along with the airport pick-up and personal drives and warm welcomes, meant for the position he had held.

Reality is cruel, you may cynically conclude.

However, truth be told, what he and all of us deserve

is really only a Styrofoam cup. It is a great lesson on Humility. And according to Simon, on Gratitude as well.

We can enjoy the perks we are given but we need to be clear that they come with our position. They do not and will not ever belong to us.

"As you gain fame, as you gain fortune, as you gain position in seniority, people will treat you better. They will hold doors open for you. They will get you a cup of tea or coffee without you even asking. They will call you "Sir" or "Ma'am" and they will give you stuff. None of that stuff is meant for you. That stuff is meant for the position you hold ... You will always deserve a Styrofoam cup."

    Simon Sinek

I'm well aware that the power I hold and the honourable welcomes I currently receive are merely temporary. They will last as long as I am in my position in MeTL.

Yes, I'm a leader under 30 who's handling a large portfolio.

Yes, I come from a family that has provided me comfort and opportunities which I have not squandered.

And yes, I may not know everything but I'm trying to learn as much as I can.

Finally, yes, I shall always remind myself to stay

humble. Because humility is a trait that garners respect. And that respect will last.

For a long, long time.

Chapter 9
Creating Our Umbrella Brand

"A brand for a company is like a reputation for a person. You earn reputation by trying to do hard things well."

— Jeff Bezos

Brand identities. Brand stories. An umbrella brand.

It all begins with a name. A brand-new brand name.

According to Steve Jobs's biography, he had come up with the name for the world's favourite tech start-up after a walk on an apple farm. To him, the name sounded "fun, spirited, and not intimidating."

Perfectly aligned with his brand personality.

The name is also easier to remember. Unlike its competitors' like "Microsoft" and "Lenovo." Which was a huge plus when it came to marketing to its audience at the very beginning.

Why the Name "MO"

I often get asked why I had decided to go with the name "MO" for my umbrella brand.

Two main reasons:

1) My brother, Mohammed "Mo" Dewji, has close-to-celebrity status in the country. He is the CEO and President of MeTL, a retired member of parliament, and Africa's youngest billionaire. His professional and philanthropic works have brought a lot of followers. So there is faith associated with this name.
2) It is short and simple to remember. Seriously, that's it!

When someone talks about MO, I want them to think of "Home."

From idea creation to manufacture, our products are made here in Tanzania, right under our brilliant sky. They are made by our fellow people. And they belong right in our homes.

I want consumers to feel that MO is a trustworthy brand that will take good care of them, that will help them fulfil their responsibilities towards their daily routines, that will do right by them and our environment.

That it stands for everything good and right.

That it supports them through both fair and bad times.

Why Umbrella Branding

If you haven't heard of the term "Umbrella Branding," it is a strategy that markets different but related products under a single brand name.

Two familiar examples of umbrella branding are: Nivea for lip balms, sunscreen lotions, body lotions etc.; and Virgin Group for media, publishing, airways, greenhouse removal, healthcare and many, many more. (And I do mean *many* more. Sir Richard Branson has founded an umbrella brand of more than 400 companies!)

At MeTL, we have about 150 products which are categorised in various groups or images. I wanted to find a way to unite them, bring them all under a family tree, so to speak.

So I dove deeper into umbrella branding and found several advantages we can definitely benefit from:

1. **It boosts efficiency.** Can you imagine running separate campaigns for our different groups of products? That's writing hundreds of copy and scripts, filming dozens of commercials, and designing countless ads. Insane and totally unnecessary! With an umbrella brand, we can gather our efforts and focus on promoting just one brand. For example, we could run a single campaign collecting customer testimonials on our various household products and link them back to MeTL. The next time a family needs to buy detergent, they'll think of us and maybe they'll also stock up on kitchen items like cooking oil, or beauty products like our soaps, too.

I want MO to be ingrained in consumers' minds so deeply that when they realise they need something for their home, from dishwashing detergent to laundry soap to cooking oil to wheat flour, or even to an air conditioner or bicycle, they'll think of us right away.

2. **It creates waves of credibility.** When one of our products receives raving reviews from our customers, the general credibility of our brand and other products will also rise. However, if our products exist in separate brands, our customers will never be able to make the connection and one product's success will remain woefully brief and limited. With an umbrella brand, we can gain more momentum and let the success ride on.

We Touch Your Life

This is why I've decided to create a fuller and more complete brand identity. Through years of reaching out and understanding my customers, I'm able to create a proper connection now. I want to make them feel like they are a part of something big.

Hence, I've come up with a slogan for all my advertising, one that would bring everything together: *Mo...Tunagusa maisha yako*, which, loosely translated from Kiswahili, means, "Mo...We touch your life."

My plan is that in five years when people see this slogan, they can immediately understand our mission and values. By seeing this slogan, they can feel connected to our company.

Much like McDonalds for example. Everyone sees the big "M" sign and they know what the company is, what it does, what the food tastes like, and how it feels to be eating their food etc.

Or if you need toothpaste, you would think of Colgate. If you need a hot, piping cup of Americano, you would think of Starbucks.

If you're a Tanzanian and you need laundry soap, or cooking oil, or a soda, or fabric for your children's clothes, or bedsheets, or a motorcycle, you'd think of us right away.

Sub-Brand Names

So why is there a need for us to have different sub-brand names under the umbrella name? Even when it's under the same category of, say, detergent?

> For example, we have three different brands for detergent. They each come with different artwork and different SKUs.
>
> 1) MO Halisi is the economic range
> 2) MO Poa is the affordable range
> 3) MO Detergent is the premium range

We've decided to group our detergent products into three sub-brands because the market is made of consumers with different economic classes and financial abilities.

Let's take a family making $200 a month. Their budget is tight so they use products under MO Halisi.

When they start to earn more money, they don't have to switch to a different brand (from another company).

They can easily upgrade or move up the value chain and use MO Poa or MO Detergent.

They can still maintain brand loyalty whether their buying power goes up or down!

Funny Story about Brand Loyalty

We have many loyal customers. But should we ever have a "Most Loyal Brand Customer" award, it will definitely go to my father.

Our products are created for the mass. Naturally, a person of Senior Dewji's means and status might choose to use other prestigious, imported brands.

But no. He refuses to use products from any other competitor. He bathes with MO mosquito repellent soap every day. At home and at the office, if he sees us using products from other companies, he would get tremendously upset.

In this weird and funny way, I've learned to be loyal to our brand from him.

You see how MO is really Home to us now?

Chapter 10
Our Social Media Story

"Work hard, learn all you can, and never miss the chance to connect with someone new."

— Amber Naslund

In our time, it would be strange if a company isn't on social media. For MeTL, as always, it was an uphill battle trying to convince the management that social media mattered.

Like everything else, our social media was an unorganized mess when we jumped in to set up our Facebook account in 2013. We had one guy posting our artwork. No story to the posts, no messages, no analysis on the reach, just a bunch of floating artwork. Basically, there was zero engagement. If you view our Facebook page, you'll see how we've evolved. I admit, it was quite funny at first.

Persuading the management to spend money on something that is on the computer screen was a great challenge. Imagine trying to convince my father that posting an ad on Facebook could potentially get us a higher reach than the number of people viewing a billboard!

In September 2014, I hired a marketing agency to handle my social media platform. It is formed by two young guys with lots of energy, vision, and drive. Now at three and a half years later, they are still running it. The journey has been incredible.

How We Connect

My social media page is not just a place for us to post our advertisements. It's also where we truly connect with people.

Here, we launched our Usikate Tamaa campaign, our Pindua Ushide campaign, and our MO margarine star campaign. People have poured their hearts out and told us their Usikate Tamaa stories. We are always moved when a new story about conquering hardship and challenges is shared.

Here, we launched MO Electro (our line of electronics) and MO Express (mini marts).

Here, we posted the mannequin challenge that resulted in over 400,000 views.

Here, we've celebrated Christmas, New Year, Eid al-Fitr, Diwali, Easter, and all national holidays with our audience over the years.

Here, we've asked our audience to send us photos of their travels with MO sodas. So far, we have photos of our drinks appearing at the peak of Mt. Kilimanjaro and even in Santorini, Greece!

The most amazing experience is when we post recipes of cakes, spaghetti with sauce, fried chicken, Mandazi (African donuts), as well as ice lollies using MO products and literally have people replying with photos of them making the food. They warm and feed our hearts.

We also tie up with celebrities such as Idris Sultan to film ads with a phone. It was a low-budget ad with Idris using MO Matchstick and cooking MO Spaghetti in a comical way. That ad went viral. So many in our audience joined in and cooked up a spaghetti storm on their side!

And finally, we use social media to empower our Tanzanian youths. We open conversations on education, healthcare, and the importance of clean drinking water. We connect to help change our side of the world.

Soon, we set up our Instagram and Twitter accounts, too. The former is used hand-in-hand with Facebook while the latter focuses on our corporate side with news on crops and the economy.

Data Doesn't Lie

Today, we have 1-1.5 million views on our posts every week. And out of those views come great comments and important feedback on our products. It's a terrific way of doing targeted market research and hearing directly from our younger audience.

From a sales and marketing standpoint, social media has been extremely helpful because now, we can quantify our reach. We have data on the number of people who have viewed our posts, as well as the sales directly obtained through social media promotion.

Social media is all about engagement. A lot of our

launches are done live so our audience can follow us in real time. Communication flows so freely. The comment section is spectacular with all the advice, feedback, and love given and reciprocated.

All of these connections wouldn't have been possible without the two amazing young lads from the marketing agency. We've been on the same wavelength since Day One. Their energy is absolutely contagious. They understand what people want. And they know how to tell great stories.

Yes, even the management is sold. Social media matters.

We Hear You

Raving reviews aren't the only things we listen to. Brutally honest feedback gets our full attention, too.

When we posted about MO Juice, our audience said that the taste was artificial. There was also a problem with the bottle caps. They were tough to open and customers would spill their drink when they used more force.

With this feedback, I recently relaunched MO Pride with flavours that had been approved by the market and fixed the packaging with a sleeker design.

Our matchstick is another product we've gotten critical comments on. Apparently, the skillets broke rather easily so we coordinated with the manufacturing team to work on making them stronger.

When our products are not being stocked in certain areas, our customers would let us know first-hand. And we would be sure to make the arrangements immediately. This is terrific because we can now identify the exact places we were not delivering before and make sure our products now reach them.

Who knew that social media could be such a great way of getting market feedback?

Exploring New Paths

Do you buy drinking water for your household? Do you buy it in bulk out of convenience?

Wouldn't you love it if a brand offers to deliver your water purchase right to your doorstep and save you from the shoulder strains and aching backs?

That's exactly what we thought of offering to our consumers. This time, however, we decided to try a new way of asking them if they would like this service.

We did a Facebook Lead Ad.

We set up a geographical target, mainly at Masaki, the city center, Kariakoo, and Upanga. People in these regions (who are on Facebook) would be asked to fill a form with their details, indicating if they wanted water delivered to their house.

To be honest, I thought it was a long shot. A bold try, sure. But a long shot.

I didn't expect people would want to change their water supplier.

But they did.

Within a month, we were able to get 60 households to start using our water. Not a one-time deal, mind you, but on a regular basis for a long term. Over the period of one year, we were able to increase the water supply to a growth of 4% directly as a result of the lead ads.

It was a resounding success!

A-One Products and Bottlers, our subsidiary, followed up with a fantastic job on the customer service front during the deliveries. Our combined efforts saw a hike in our water unit sales!

We are "The People's Brand"

Wherever people go, we go. No doubt social media platforms are where we'll be spending more marketing efforts on as well. There's so much feedback to gather without us going from retailer to retailer. Now we're interacting directly with a big group of our customers. And so far, the response has been delightful.

Chapter 11
Giving Back

"To move forward, you have to give back."

— Oprah Winfrey

My father is a strong personality, but he is also very humble.

He is all about helping the community and giving back. I don't think he has ever turned away anyone who has come to ask for help.

And if you spot my parents on the streets of Tanzania, you would never be able to tell that they are wealthy. Not in the way they dress. Not in the way they act.

That's one of the many things I love about them. They choose to remain humble inside out. They choose to drill into us the belief that "No one is ever beneath us."

Bearing fully in mind this critical lesson on humility from my parents, we at MeTL have also decided to carry out some Corporate Social Responsibility (CSR). To help take care of our people and environment, wherever and whenever we can.

For it would be useless if a company prospers while the people it serves, our fellow Tanzanians, are suffering.

Filthy Water Is Killing Us

According to Water.Org, around 27 million of Tanzanians lack access to clean water and around 35 million lack access to improved sanitation.

One of our major health concerns here is Cholera. It is a diarrhoeal infection caused by food and water that have been contaminated with Vibrio cholera, a bacterium. This is an acute infection that can affect children and adults. Left untreated, patients might very possibly die.

The World Health Organization puts the number of cholera cases in Tanzania between 15 August 2015 and 7 January 2018 at 33, 421, including 542 deaths.

A fatality rate of 1.62%.

People are dying because they don't have clean water. Worse, many of them don't know about the dangers of polluted water and still drink or feed them to their children!

Within the two years since we started, my team and I have run five campaigns to educate fellow Tanzanians on the risks of drinking and using dirty water.

Many of them thought, Water is water. It doesn't need to be that clean. What is purification, anyway? Why must we do that?

We needed to make sure we were getting in their minds and changing their understanding of water-borne diseases as well as the importance of clean water.

To establish credibility in our message and gain more trust, I made sure we had a doctor on board. We set off on our own road show and travelled around to talk about clean drinking water and how to obtain it.

This campaign reached more than one million people in Dar and the coastal region within 28 days. It has now become one of our top company events. Every year, we resolve to see it through. It is that important to us.

Because we believe that only through a change in understanding can there be a change in behaviour.

And only through a change in behaviour can there be a firm breakaway from unnecessary fatality.

1.62% is way too high.

Let's bring it down together.

Cleaning Up

Another great initiative we've brought about in Tanzania is helping to clean up the environment.

As a company of Fast Moving Consumer Goods, our products are mostly packaged in plastic. It hurts us to think that our bottles and containers, discarded upon use, are clogging our environment and killing marine life.

Hence in 2012, we installed a plastic recycling plant

to make sure we are doing our part in reducing plastic in the waste stream and controlling plastic pollution.

Part of our previous "Under the Cap" promotion campaign was to raise awareness about the effects of trash on the environment. As a step towards encouraging the concept of recycling, we awarded cash prizes to people who collected empty plastic bottles to recycle at our plant.

On a proud note, it wasn't that difficult to get Tanzanians onboard. Our country has become very environmentally conscious.

On the 54th anniversary of Tanzania's independence, our president, Dr. John Pombe Magufuli, made it a national "clean up" day. The campaign was to raise awareness about keeping the environment clean and averting health hazards such as cholera. The government has since announced that every first Saturday of the month be dedicated to cleaning up our beautiful land.

Going out there and cleaning up with our staff made us realise just how much trash was in our environment. And now, we as a company can play a bigger part in treating the place we live in with more love and more kindness.

How One Woman's Bravery Helps Hundreds of Thousands of Girls

In 2016, I was fortunate enough to interview Hyasintha Ntuyeko, founder of Kasole Secrets, a Tanzanian company that specialises in organic sanitary pads and pantyliners. She opened my eyes on how one woman can affect more people to step up and speak for all Tanzanian girls and women.

On a topic that is crucial yet has been treated as a taboo for generations: Menstrual hygiene.

In our culture, nobody talks about periods and the discomfort a young woman has to experience every month. Mothers never talk about them. And so, daughters learn not to.

To publicly discuss the problems we face during our menstrual cycles is considered "shameful."

Problems like not having access to safe-quality sanitary pads, clean water, clean toilets to change the pads in, and proper disposal bins are kept buried at the back of everyone's mind and pretended as the most trivial inconvenience.

On average, Tanzanian girls miss out 41 days of school in a year because of these problems (on top of menstrual cramps, which, by the way, are *very* real and *very* painful). Without sanitary pads and clean toilet facilities in schools, they can only stay at home. Imagine having to miss lessons just because your environment disagrees with you having your period!

After she graduated from university, Hyasintha went from selling sanitary pads to setting up her own business producing Glory Girl (sanitary pads made from bamboo charcoal) and bravely speaking up about this "taboo topic."

What We're Doing

At MeTL, we have our own line of sanitary pads called "Mo Princess." I want girls and young women to feel dignified and treasured on those days we feel most uncomfortable. We deserve to.

On a bigger, practical level, we are now partnering with the Mo Dewji Foundation to build clean toilets for girls. We are also giving out sanitary pads in schools so that they won't have to miss lessons during their periods.

Then on a more personal level, inspired by Hyasintha's movement to raise awareness on menstrual hygiene, I've also started a campaign to educate both boys and girls about it.

Why include boys?

Because children hitting puberty are highly curious about the changes involving their bodies. Getting them educated makes this no longer a topic that is "hush-hush" or "shameful," but something that is natural, and which requires consideration for the girls.

Periods are uncomfortable. Girls deserve more support from their parents, schools, and the community in making their monthly cycles as manageable as possible.

Talking about it is a start. Then comes solving some of those problems.

And I want to make sure I am a part of that.

Chapter 12
The Woman Who Empowered Me

"Your passion is for you, your purpose is for others. Your passion makes you happy. But when you use your passion to make a difference in someone else's life, that's a service, that's a purpose, and that's the hand."

– Jay Shetty

At the beginning of this book, I told you my father's story.

Now that we're coming to the end, I want to tell you the story about a woman who has inspired him his whole life.

And who, in turn, has also inspired me.

Clever and resilient, my grandmother lived with wholehearted passion.

Maa, the Woman Ahead of Her Time

It was 1921.

In our culture, men are the breadwinners. Hence, a Muslim hijabi woman with no formal education like Maa should have stayed at home to look after her family. That was all.

Except, it was precisely that reason—to feed and take care of her family, that Maa went out to work. She would stitch clothes for money then invest it into her shop.

A woman "working."

For money. Which she used to "invest."

Into "her shop."

These were concepts and terms that people in that generation couldn't understand. But Maa went straight for them!

When misery sets in, it's normal for people to feel sorry for themselves and to give up. Not Maa, though. The tougher the times, the harder she worked.

She had this peculiar resilience, a certain attitude, to go after what she wanted. She understood her value and purpose with a clarity that would have blinded others.

And that attitude has been passed on to all of us Dewjis.

The inspiration behind Educate, Empower & Inspire (EEI) came from her. I believe there are many women out there who have the abilities, the talents, and the drive like Maa had.

But they need a little motivation or help to get started or to grow and become great.

In every generation, in every person, there is always a struggle. It could be a struggle to feed your family. It could be a struggle to prove your worth at work. It could be a struggle to find a job you really love.

My grandmother struggled with plenty of problems. But she chose to own those struggles. She chose to search for the light inside her even at the darkest of times.

If she hadn't, my father wouldn't be the man he is. And he wouldn't have instilled these qualities of perseverance and humility into us.

And we wouldn't have been able to play a bigger part in our society.

Everything would have been different if that one woman hadn't allowed her spirit to shine through the cracks and let it trickle down to the next generations.

I see now that this is what I'm here for.

To let my grandmother's indomitable spirit shine through me. Then let *my* work cast some light on people who need it.

The Time Life Stank & How I Turned It Around

You probably don't know this but up until the age of 15, I did not have my life together.

I believed that I was not capable of being smart, successful, and driven. I had convinced myself that I was not "worthy" and could never be.

I was always told I was average, always criticised for not being good enough. So for a long time, that was what I believed, too.

I made excuses. I constantly felt sorry for myself and gave up when things didn't go my way.

One day, I was sitting at the school assembly, watching my friends go onstage to receive academic awards. There was a huge pit in my stomach because I was so tired of feeling like I'd fallen short, that I would never catch up or make it.

Till this day, I would never know what ticked in me that day. But in one incredible moment, I made the most important decision of my life, one that would turn things around.

I decided I would do whatever it took to make sure I was up on that stage the following semester.

Whatever it took.

Believe me, it took A LOT.

Studying was the easy part. What was tedious was fighting with my mind every day in believing that I could do this. My main battle was to drown out the noise of the people who didn't believe in me and to dedicate myself 100%.

Every time I felt like giving up, I envisioned a life in which I was a success.

"Just a little bit more, just a little bit longer," I would remind myself.

I stood on that stage finally.

I completed high school at the top of my class and graduated from Georgetown University.

I played golf competitively and was the only Muslim girl on the team.

I was an average 15-year-old who had the courage to believe her will could overcome any challenge or obstacle Life threw at her.

And I went to step on many more bigger stages.

Nobody Wants to Climb the Mountain

It's funny. I'm often told that I got life easy.

When people look at me, they see the titles or definitions of my identity—The capable businesswoman; the golfer; the motivational speaker.

What they don't see are the 90-hour work week, the hours I would spend on the golf course every single day just to perfect my swing, or the 'N' number of times I had to give up a night out with my friends because I had to study…only to wake at 5 a.m. to do it all over again.

They don't see the weekends I had to stay in to prepare for my speeches. They don't see the number of times I've failed, and how I've had to force myself to get up because I knew people were counting on me.

Like customers browsing our shelves, outsiders often see the product and not the manufacturing process. (Who wants to anyway?)

Everyone wants to reach the summit, but no one wants to climb the mountain. (Again, who wants to?)

For me, I climb the mountain every day. Because I know it's the only way to reach the summit instead of dreaming about it.

Bill Gates. Steve Jobs. Oprah Winfrey. Messi or Ronaldo (if you are a Madrid fan). These are the people who have failed time and time again. But they've always picked themselves up and kept going. They are committed. They are resilient. That's why they are unstoppable.

And I'm now following their footsteps.

So When Does the Magic Happen?

Ah, the magic of success.

I believe it happens when you start to believe in yourself, when you start to value who you are, when you understand that your voice and actions matter.

That's the first spark of magic.

Then the actual burst happens when you begin to understand that it's not all about you. That it's really about finding a purpose bigger than just you.

That means serving others.

Helping others overcome a particular problem. Helping others achieve a specific dream.

That's what I want to do.

One Inspired Dreamer at a Time

With Educate, Empower & Inspire, I hope to change or move the world. My team and I absolutely believe that everyone has the capacity to fulfil their dreams.

With the right tools and mentorship, all of us can get there.

Including you.

Especially you.

If you're looking for guidance or a dose of motivation to keep you on your track of success, come check out what we have produced. Our self-development articles, videos, and e-books are created for serious dreamers like you. Our show puts influential women in the spotlight, so you can get a glimpse of how they are making a difference in our communities.

I sincerely hope you take the first step towards fulfilling your own dream.

I sincerely hope you find the courage to reach out and seek all the resources you can get.

I sincerely hope you live and love your life as passionately as you can.

Like *Maa* did. We need more people like her in our world.

We need you.

NOTES

Chapter 1:
1. Quinteros, Michelle. "Bill Gates Quote—20 Sayings That Prove Success Starts Within." *Quotezine*. 2013. quotezine.com/bill-gates-quotes-20-sayings-that-prove-success-starts-within/.
2. McGowan, Michael. "How Roger Bannister and Australian John Landy raced to break the four-minute mile." *The Guardian*. Guardian Media Group, 5 March 2018. theguardian.com/sport/2018/mar/05/how-roger-bannister-and-australian-john-landy-raced-to-break-the-four-minute-mile.
3. "The 12 men who walked on the moon." *Mach*. NBC News Digital. Updated 28 May 2018. nbcnews.com/mach/science/12-men-who-walked-moon-ncsl707951

Chapter 2:
1. Jean, Wyclef. "Dreaming Beyond Limitations." Interview with Tom Bilyeu, Impact Theory. 21 February 2017. Video Interview.

Chapter 3:
1. Robbins, Mel. "Why Motivation is Garbage." Interview with Tom Bilyeu, Impact Theory. 31 January 2017. Video Interview.
2. Tolkien, J. R. R.. *The Lord of the Rings*. Great Britain: HarperCollins Publishers, 2004. Paperback.
3. Lao Tzu. *Tao Te Ching*. Chapter 64. Translated by Lin Yutang, 1948.

Chapter 4:
1. Banayan, Alex. "How to Hack Your Way into Success at Anything." Interview with Tom Bilyeu, Impact Theory. 26 June 2018. Video Interview.
2. Sinek, Simon. "Start with Why: How Great Leaders Inspire Action." TEDxPuget Sound. TED Talk, September 2009. Video.
3. "Shetta."Wikipedia. Last edited 25 June 2018. en.wikipedia.org/wiki/Shetta.
4. Clements, Cecil. *Corporate Capsules: Three Simple Steps for Corporate Success*. Chennai: Notion Press, 2016.

Chapter 5:
1. Meah, Asad. "50 Inspirational Nelson Mandela Quotes That Will Change Your Life." *Awaken the Greatness Within*. awakenthegreatnesswithin.com/50-inspirational-nelson-mandela-quotes-that-will-change-your-life/.
2. Bies, Robert J, Ph.D. Professor of Management and Founder and First Academic Director of the Executive Master's in Leadership Program at the McDonough School of Business. Georgetown University. *This is the quote I heard from my professor for years!
3. Yunus, Dr. Muhammad. Social entrepreneur, economist, and founder of Grameen Bank. To learn more about Dr. Yunus, check out his Nobel Prize biography:

nobelprize.org/prizes/peace/2006/yunus/biographical/
4. "Tanzania: 1.5 Million Adolescents Not in School." Human Rights Watch. 14 February 2017. hrw.org/news/2017/02/14/tanzania-15-million-adolescents-not-school.
5. "What We've Learnt from the National Survey on Child Marriage in Tanzania." Girls Not Brides. 4 April 2017. girlsnotbrides.org/weve-learnt-national-survey-child-marriage-tanzania/.
6. Johnson, Inquoris "Inky." Learn more about Inky's story and works here: inkyjohnson.com/about/.

Chapter 6:
1. "John C. Maxwell Quotes About Values." AZQuotes. azquotes.com/author/9639-John_C_Maxwell/tag/values.

Chapter 7:
1. Hardy, Benjamin P.. "23 Michael Jordan Quotes That Will Immediately Boost Your Confidence." Inc.. 5 April 2016. inc.com/benjamin-p-hardy/23-michael-jordan-quotes-that-will-immediately-boost-your-confidence.html.

Chapter 8:
1. Harder, Lori. "How to Go From Rock Bottom to the Top." Interview with Tom Bilyeu, Impact Theory. 5 June 2018. Video Interview.

2. UshersNewLook. "5 Rules to Follow As You Find Your Spark by Simon Sinek." Online video clip. *Youtube,* 17 October 2016. Web.

Chapter 9:
1. Meah, Asad. "47 Inspirational Jeff Bezos Quotes on Success." *Awaken the Greatness Within.* awakenthegreatnesswithin.com/47-inspirational-jeff-bezos-quotes-on-success/.
2. Isaacson, Walter. *Steve Jobs.* New York: Simon & Schuster, 2011. Hardcover.
3. Learn more about NIVEA here: nivea.co.uk/about-us/our-company/brand-and-company.
4. Learn more about Virgin Group here: virgin.com/virgingroup/content/about-us.

Chapter 10:
1. Leaning, Brittany. "25 Must-Tweet Inspirational Quotes from Inbound Experts." HubSpot, Inc.. Last updated 28 July 2017. blog.hubspot.com/marketing/inspirational-quotes-inbound-experts.

Chapter 11:
1. Stanford Report. "Oprah talks to graduates about feelings, failure and finding happiness." Edited transcript of Oprah Winfrey's speech at Stanford's Commencement ceremony. Stanford News. 15 June 2008. news.stanford.edu/news/2008/june18/como-061808.html

2. "Tanzania's water and sanitation crisis." Water.Org. Last checked 7 September 2018. water.org/our-impact/tanzania/
3. "Cholera – United Republic of Tanzania." Disease Outbreak News, World Health Organization. 12 January 2018. who.int/csr/don/12-january-2018-cholera-tanzania/en/.
4. "Tanzanian president John Magufuli cleans streets on Independence Day." Deutsche Welle. DW.com. 9 December 2015. dw.com/en/tanzanian-president-john-magufuli-cleans-streets-on-independence-day/a-18907686.
5. Fatema Dewji. "Fatema Dewji - Jaffer Interview with Hyasintha Ntuyeko." Online video clip. Youtube, 27 April 2016. Web.

Chapter 12:
1. Shetty, Jay. "How to Find Your Purpose." Interview with Tom Bilyeu, Impact Theory. 20 February 2018. Video Interview.
2. To learn more about Educate, Empower & Inspire, check out: empoweredwithfatema.com/.

ABOUT THE AUTHOR

An avid golfer since she was six years old, Fatema Dewji grew up in Tanzania and went to Georgetown University for her undergraduate studies in Finance and Management. In 2010, she started working at MeTL (Mohammed Enterprises Tanzania Limited), one of the largest business houses in Africa.

She is the marketing head of MeTL and founder of Educate, Empower & Inspire—a platform she uses to inspire those around her. With burning passion and gentle warmth, she has launched a series of videos on Marketing and Leadership with topics that include: Focusing on your customers; maintaining a connection with your consumers; the makings of great leaders; and finding your purpose in business as well as in your personal life. Her other videos cover motivational messages of gratitude, self-worth, and emotional resilience. She has also conducted over 50 interviews with fascinating people from different backgrounds. Her vision is to make a difference globally.

This is a book for two special groups:

Those who want to find someone to inspire them.

And those who want to inspire others.

> fatemadewji.co.tz
> @fatemadewji
> #aheadoftheherd

www.ingramcontent.com/pod-product-compliance
Lightning Source LLC
Chambersburg PA
CBHW031428210526
45464CB00005B/2108